BARE NAKED TREES

By
Rachel S. Morrison

"There is something simplistically common in all of us..."

Printed in the U.S.A. by Createspace.com

BARE NAKED TREES

In loving memory of my angels who continue to shine love and wisdom on me everywhere I go to make sure that I am guided confidently down the roads that lead me to Bare Naked Trees...

Contents

Contents

Acknowledgements

I am so grateful for the grace that has been given me. I am so very honored and humbled that God chose me. I know that without Your love, forgiveness, and guidance, I would not be successful. I thank You and love You, God with all my heart and soul.

I want to thank my two sons (big one and little one, even though you both are bigger than me now!) for always having faith in me and motivating me to complete my dreams. You are the lights that shine for me whenever it is dark; even in the daylight. I am full because I have your smiles, memories and beautiful hearts to keep me. I love you and pray only the best for you and that you find your passion in life to live where your dreams can take you! And to my future daughter in law, I thank you for being an awesome mother to my adorable grandson! I know the hard work you put in! Nah Nah loves you, K!

Thanks to my mom (Hi, Mommie!) who showed me by example how to keep pushing onward no matter what is in front of me. Thank you for being the one constant cheerleader in my life. I love you!

Thanks to both of my grandmas for their

unconditional love and support. They helped instill the confidence and courage in me to make sure that I love myself before each day's end and to always embrace my particular persona. Grandma, I thank you for the strength in the fight you took for me so that I didn't have to. I love you and miss you immensely!

Thanks to my big sister RM, who is an author and poet in her own right, for unselfishly taking the time to edit and help put the finishing touches on this project without any complaints (well besides the commas!) We have come a long way to get our own *Bare Naked Trees* and the best part is we found a lot of them together. Let's promise to continue to pick up the rest of our leaves!

Thanks to my younger sister RM, who although we are close in age (we were really never twins!) At times we have been like two peas in a pod trying to learn our way. I thank you for always being okay with who I am. (But, you are still not the Diva!)

Thanks to my baby sister RM, for always being true to who you are no matter what! (Girl, Bye!) We've got more left to do and more leaves to gather.

Thanks to my aunties and uncles who helped instill education and life lessons that were instrumental in helping me become the scholar, writer, and aunty woman that I am today. Thank you for stepping up and accepting that it truly takes a village.

Thanks to all of my nieces and nephews (all 100 million of ya'll!), for your love and support and for humoring me by celebrating my birthday for the whole month every year. I love being your aunty! Be ready next year. It don't stop!

Thanks to JP, for mentoring me and giving me the space to grow and become the professional that I am. Thanks for having an open mind and heart to continue to do the work that you do.

Thanks to my colleagues and everyone who has been a part of my growth and life learning. I truly appreciate you!

And lastly, thank you to my angel JRG. I know you didn't think I'd forget to shout you out! I miss you deep within my soul. I wish you were here to experience this with me because you would be so proud and smiling from ear to ear. I love you! I know that you are always watching over me making sure to tuck me in at night safely with my *Bare Naked Trees*.

Intrologue

Bare Naked Trees **and its contents is not meant to serve as a therapeutic intervention or practice and only attempts to offer options of self-reflection and self-healing. It is intended not to promote or replace any spiritual or religious following. Know that *You* are the one who holds the key to unlock the chest to your personal happiness and success. If you *believe* in your truth, *you* have all you need to get to your own *Bare Naked Trees*.**

Preface

"There is something simplistically common in all of us when we are naked and standing in front of a mirror. It is the only time in the day that we cannot run or hide. Not even from ourselves. Whether you choose to see you or not, you are who you are and it is what it is."

*****

We are all on a quest to become the best at something while we work on improving who we are and how or where we fit in. So for this conversation while we begin to talk about change and how we view change in our lives, Bare Naked Trees discusses many things in between that lend to our ultimate journey, our uniqueness, and our movement towards positive progress.

From figuring out change in adversity, to new opportunities. From different relationships that love can create, to recognizing the moments during and after change takes shape that can influence or discourage us with the choices which we have made.

If we can begin to accept that wherever we came from was the perfect place for our story to begin, then in change, we can choose what we let about our upbringing, our accomplishments, even others opinions of us, be the deciding factor of how we value our self-worth.

Bare Naked Trees is meant to be that nudging positive voice of 'real talk' that keeps one's self-confidence at a level so high above the scale, that when you hear the voice of doubt saying, "You are not worthy of a great relationship," or, "You are not good enough for the finer things in life," you will not hesitate to silence it.

If you yearn for the understanding of what people are talking about when they speak about unconditional self-love or self-acceptance, then these words are meant to be the mirror holding the reflection for you to see that true love and self-admiration is inside of you, and, only you hold the answers to your success.

You see, as cliché as it may sound, we all know it is not really about the shape of your face, the texture of your hair, or the length of your legs. It has never been about the size of your ears or the amount of fat on your body that determines who you are or what potential you have.

It always has and always will have to do with how much confidence, trust, and courage we have in ourselves to be able to do decide the best course of action we must take every time a new situation requires. Bare Naked Trees is meant to help you meet YOU wherever you are in your life or in your process of change, so then you can make sure that everything about you stays on the course which was custom tailored with only you in mind.

Maybe your story has nothing to do with your ability to work with immediate change because you have figured out that you can do that very well. But instead, it is that your story could be in your past you were not allowed to express your opinions, so today, you still allow the voice of low self-esteem to tell you that you should move to the back where you cannot be noticed.

Then, Bare Naked Trees is here to give you the okay you need to yell out as loud as you want to about what is right for you.

Or maybe your story could be that the only way anger was expressed in your home was for your mother or father to take their frustrations out on you by knocking you upside your head every time you turned around, and now as a parent, you find yourself abusing your own children.

So right now, at this moment, Bare Naked Trees may have just the words that you need to help you take a look at you and your anger to keep you from passing those damaging ways of coping with life on to the next generation of you.

It could just be that you have reached a point in your life where you know it is time for change, but you need the tools and a little assistance with where to start.

Then, Bare Naked Trees is here to give you the confidence to help put things in perspective so that you can be the change you want in your life.

You just have to see it! Believe it! To live it!

Preface Reflection

*You are who you are. If you don't believe in you, no one else will. It's time to show up."

*What is your reason or reasons for change?

*Are you ready to put in the work required for change?

Chapter One
Positive Process of Change

*****

While I don't confess to know it all, I have learned that life is mostly about making choices and facing change, some which will be challenging and hard to deal with. From the time that you were able to explore your surroundings you had to make a choice of which way to go. And when things changed in your life you had to find some way to figure out how to deal with that change.

Because it is true when something has to change in our lives, or when some unexpected event causes us to have to dig deep inside to the bare essentials of everything that we are comfortable with, we have choices. We either stand, put our game face on, and brace for the competition with whatever it is that we are familiar with. Or, we resist and fight the new reality. Or, we become brave enough to seek the new tools needed, hit the problem head on, and confidently keep it moving.

Or, if when we are caught off guard and find ourselves unprepared for the flexibility that change demands when it comes, we give someone else our power to decide for us while we run as fast as we can until there is nowhere else to run, and we are then back to where we first started only to meet the challenge waiting for us again right where we initially left it.

Either way, and regardless of what we believe, we can only run as far as the air in our lungs will allow us, and only as high as our beliefs will take us. Because change, regardless of its magnitude, whether it be large or small, may be necessary to create a new way of thinking going forward that requires new rules and a new type of standard.

This can depend on our level of personal success that we have attained in our lives at the time of change. Especially if we have other factors to deal with such as children, a stressful job, or a failing marriage or relationship, mental deficits, or violence in our homes; not to mention many other life stressors which can weigh upon us.

It seems that when change comes in one category of our lives such as a new promotion, we tend to apply the changes only to that particular column and move about in all other areas of our lives as if the change shouldn't be attached to the full circle.

I believe in order for us to get this thing right, we must open our minds to acquire a better understanding that the *process of change* deserves a certain kind of passion in patience, and commands a certain amount of settling in that only time can give us. This time is needed in order to create a significant shift that needs to occur with change.

The emphasis put on the style of clothes that we wear, what color heeled shoes we buy, what types of car we drive, the food we eat, or where we choose to live, continue to make it hard for some of us to put it all aside and shine when outer beauty doesn't matter; like in times of true adversity.

Look. We all have stuff that we have to work on with ourselves, but it has to come to a time where enough is enough with making excuses for our behaviors or blaming our short comings on our parents, on failed relationships, or on bad decisions that we have made. It is time to just be real with getting better at working on those unhealthy sides of us that are detrimental to the fabric of who we really are. It is your responsibility to figure out how to do you with what you have been given. It is your responsibility to find out what you need to get it done sooner than later.

So is true to the process, as I pondered for months as to what type of reading *Bare Naked Trees* should actually be. Should it be about asking more questions than getting answers? If we are going to talk about love, self-love, self-acceptance, self-worth, and our purpose?

Should it be a culmination of stories about love? Or about how the relationship between oneself and love is developed, and how is that relationship nourished and then kept sacred? Where do we get the tools to help us stay courageously strong in fear? And, where do we even start?

Well, finally after having a few conversations about all of this, I still had only come up with a few instances where self-love was even mentioned. I knew that I had to take this conversation to others to see what they thought about some of these topics. It wasn't long before I began to see striking similarities between people of all ages, different cultures, and different educational and socio-economic backgrounds. What surfaced was that when the discussion transitioned from change to talking about self-love, the stories were extremely similar. These conversations brought home the fact that it doesn't matter the face or the place, self-love or self-acceptance in general is a tough conversation to have, let alone add change to the mix.

So I am going to get up close and personal with you through *Bare Naked Trees* to show how relevant past experiences in our lives are and how they can be contributing factors to why it is harder for some than it is for others to grasp the idea that even when things change in our lives, our true self-worth lies within the connection that we have to our beliefs, the relationships that we have with ourselves, and the depth of our self-acceptance.

Because we grow accustomed to doing today the same way that we did yesterday, we bank on tomorrow not being much different. That's where I want you to stop and take a look at your yesterday. This entails looking at your relationship with your parents, your children, siblings, friends, and lastly your relationship with yourself to make sure that you are okay. So that if something just isn't right in your heart about *you*, you stop ignoring it, put it on notice, and dedicate the next year to getting *you* right with *you*. No matter about your past, tomorrow can have a better shine to it and you've got to be ready for it.

I want you to feel like now is the time to start putting self-doubt and self-blame down, and start accepting that you deserve to do better for yourself, those whom you love, and for those who love you.

Since most of us look to what others are doing to define the standard of beauty for the season, we let the sometimes slanted view of reality and entertainment shows convince us that our own fabulousness and inner strength is not good enough. We've fallen into the trap of believing that it is easier to look into the lives of others and let them tell us yes or no regarding our dress.

But I believe that we all have inside of us the power to decide that if we treat ourselves like we really want and deserve to be treated, everyone else around us will follow our lead and move out of our way. We have to believe that self-love, true forgiveness, and true acceptance of the differences of others is the key to living each day with true substance.

I can hear you saying, "All right. But *Naked* though? Where is she going with all of this? And more importantly, she hasn't seen my thighs!"

And you are right. I haven't seen your thighs. But you will see very soon that I understand what you question. It's not as if I have been running around my entire life "oohing" or "aahing" and winking at myself in front of every mirror that I walk by! But I must say that the concept is in a way the very essence of what this conversation of our personal journey should be.

You see, since we've started out from day one trying to fit into and live inside the mold of the life that others carve out for us, it is very important for us to start to give ourselves permission to allow our own characters to explode before we reach a level of self-sabotage that could take years of therapy to undue. Or even worse, we could become stagnant in it.

It seems that most of us spend our lives trying to achieve that nice shape and pretty face, and by the time we are well into adulthood we are left compromising not just our bank accounts trying to get to that standard of beauty, but we compromise and sacrifice who we *are* trying to get to it as well.

My hope is that, when you have finished with your *Bare Naked Trees*, the level of trust that you will have in yourself will be so insurmountable, that you will reach out as wide and high as you can and take the room needed to be who you are meant to be.

I want you to believe that you can elevate the standards and quality of your life to equal your worth. It is essential to stand in who you are, to embrace hope, believe in the power of positive aspirations, and be full of renewed spirit in your *positive process of change* and personal growth. We need to know that in the *positive process of change* we can create the room needed to accept the things that we cannot change, build the courage to change the things that we can, and then store the wisdom that we have gained to remember the difference.

Maybe some of you will say, "Nah. This is not for me. And besides, there are many ways that one can figure this all out without being naked or talking about trees." And I do agree. There are other ways to figure you out for sure. But before you make the decision to put this book down and move on, take a moment to be really honest with yourself and the way that you have been choosing to live your life and let me ask you this.

If you like many, when you are all alone changing into, let's say your pajamas, inadvertently catch a glimpse of yourself in the mirror out of the corner of your eye, get that feeling of being exposed; even if no one else is around...you grab something to cover up because you have issues with who you are; you need to recognize that you have become the person who has allowed li fe to capture a still picture of you hiding in the shadows of your existence.

Maybe you should continue to read down a few more lines so that you can figure out since you have decided that your body is too fat, or too skinny, or too ugly even for you to look at on the *outside*, how then are you ever going to illustrate the essence of how beautiful a person you really are on the *inside*? When will you allow the real self-portrait of you to step into your purpose and blossom within the abundant canvas of life that is promised you? If you are the person afraid to claim your own place, how will you be able to allow yourself the space that you need to mold your style behind your smile?

Ask yourself as we move on, have you allowed the events of your past, whatever that time was like for you, to represent you and shape your present and your future? Are you okay living the life that you have built for you and your family? And finally, no matter the time, day, job, city, automobile, or relationship that you are in, do you truly love you even in the middle of it all?

Well, it's okay if you don't have all of the answers to these questions for yourself right now, because if you are still with me this far, we can grab this moment together to find the answers on the other side of your *positive process of change*.

I say you ARE worth the time to find out!

Decide today to be willing, strong, and open enough to stop for a moment to truly appreciate you and all that you have accomplished thus far and, all that you still can do. You can do the work that is necessary for you to live your power step by step and prayer by prayer so that you can see that *the Power is in you* to be whom you want to be!

Let's push full steam ahead and get started doing the work necessary so that on this journey you will be proud to bring every piece of you along on your terms, down your own road of *Bare Naked Trees.*

Chapter Reflection

*Stay focused in change. When you make the decision stick with it. Do not waver.

*Is there change needed in your life?

*What do you need to do to get change started in your life?

Chapter Two
Interlude on Journaling

*****

While going through your *Positive Process of Change* you have to acknowledge the power of writing things down and how imperative keeping a paper trail of the journey to your personal success will be. Journaling can help you keep a real check on the projects that you need to spend your time working on daily, versus those projects that can wait until the weekend, next year, or never.

In order to help you stay focused, it is important to have something to look back on in times when life seems to lead you toward a path that is not your own, and to help keep you current with your here and now.

Keeping a diary or journal of some type to be able to go back and read about your own wants and desires will keep you on track and allow you to use yourself as a great self-motivator. It is important to record your promises so that you can remember to reflect or rejoice on your past accomplishments, your blessings, and mistakes.

Because life can seem to go bye quickly at times you don't want to have an idea or plan that you didn't get to because you forgot about it or didn't write it down.

So if you don't already have a journal, go out and purchase one and enter today's date and just start writing.

It doesn't matter what you write. Just write down whatever comes to your mind. Then give yourself a reminder to write in it again the next day, but try not to look at the notes from the day before. Just write. Commit to doing this every day. Either in the morning, or at the end of your day. Even in the middle of the night if you want to.

You will see that by the end of the week you will have a new and personal best friend that will always be there to hold your sacred memories and desires.

Within a few months' time you will start to notice what means the most to live the life that you dream of. Sounds nice right? It is. Don't be surprised if soon you have more than one.

Chapter Three
Living with Acceptance...

"Trust that the universe is interested in what you've got. Being okay with the shape of your lips, or the curve of your hips, and knowing that if someone doesn't like them, it is simply their preference that is in question, not your flaw."

*****

Along this journey that is the *process of positive change,* you will see that you are custom fitted to be just as you are. Yes. You have already been given the perfect persona. The only thing left is for you to nurture it and let it shine.

In other words, during your *positive process of change,* you can take the opportunity to look inside of you to see what you really like and what really makes you smile and then, find the tools to help build the foundation to do just that.

While *Bare Naked Trees* is a conversation about change, it is also meant to take this conversation to the places that may be tough for some of us to accept and acknowledge about ourselves; but is essential to where we must go to get to where our passion lies.

Acceptance is about deciding to take the steps to learning who you are, what your needs and desires are, and after that, seeing who you are, and being okay with it all. Once you get to know your true personality and the things that you like about you, you can decide to work toward the future that you want and start to take the necessary steps to get to it.

It is important for you to remember and recognize that you are created to be you all of the time because you already have the perfect silhouette with the flattering shadow.

Because our travels in life up until now can be used as a filter to help us decide what we hold on to and what we leave behind. Whether you approve or disapprove, whether you like or dislike, acceptance is about letting go of the events in your past and being free in it. We must begin to accept that the past is in its proper place.

Digesting the truth about who you are no matter how disgusting the taste it may leave in your mouth is what you are going to have to do to see the connection between how you sit at the table with rejection, disappointments, compliments, accomplishments, and self-acceptance. And when we talk about acceptance during this *positive process of change*, we need to understand that we are talking about acceptance of all that life has dealt us. Acceptance starts first with acknowledgement and ownership of all of you.

During your journey of positive change you will find that there is so much more to your story that you have to discover in order to move into your future with a new perspective. Acceptance in your positive change requires a willingness to go to a new level of commitment that you must first promise to stay true to, and then give yourself the permission to love you no matter how you look or what you uncover about you on the other side.

It is time to move about selfishly where you are concerned and start to think differently about you so that you can make more sound decisions about what you deserve. And, if you are currently in denial about how serious it is for your positive change to start, that's okay. Real positive change will *demand* that you go below the surface of your current existence to bury the fakeness that has falsely taken care of you up until now. And then accept that as well.

More often than not, in our lives it turns out that the stuff that we decided not to deal with or hoped would stay in the closet, is the stuff that comes back to embarrass us, stop us in our tracks, and aides in crushing our dreams.

Things like anger, regret, fear, and those

pieces of should've-would've-could'ves that should have been thrown out a long time ago at some of those pit stops along the way; as this is the stuff that eats away at our true identity. The stuff that deters the celebration of all that we have accomplished. It is the stuff that continues to add to the negative barriers that stop us from finding the extra push we need to continue to prosper.

It is true that we are all given the beautiful gift of time and new opportunities every day to correct our mistakes and start all over again. The icing on the cake will be for you to believe that even with your flaws, you have every right to focus the attention more on you.

In the journey of trying to understand this *positive process of change*, no matter what area of our lives the change occurs in, it's going to take a lot of getting to know one's real self and a lot of re-examining the way that we have been accustomed to doing things.

Along the way you will also discover that in change it takes a lot of accepting of what we find out about ourselves, our families and friends, and a lot of accepting of the decisions that we have made in our lives up until now.

During your process of change you will need to determine where tolerance and trust of yourself fit into your definition of acceptance and find out if you have a hard time trusting yourself so that you can understand where you must start to build.

I want you to understand that self-acceptance is directly related to how you treat yourself, especially after failure. For instance, after you have failed at something you have to assess how you feel about yourself. Do you beat yourself up, or do you shrug your shoulders and bounce right back when life doesn't seem to be kind to you?

The beauty of looking at you through the lens of acceptance during your *positive process of change,* is that you can decide to rewrite some of your story and incorporate only those lessons that you need from your past into your future. Figuring you out is going to require all the lessons of courage, disappointments, loss, love, mistakes, and acceptance that you can gather up about you.

Today in change, the hour has come for you to be honest, accept, and listen to what your heart is saying to you. And if you don't like how things are, or if you are not doing the things that you want or need to be doing at this juncture in your life, it's time to assign the time that is needed to change the way you handle you.

Begin to talk the talk and walk the walk, because what you say from now on is going to be

as important as what you do in *change.*

Chapter Reflection

*If you stop and think about it, figuring you out is not that complicated. You just have to begin.

*Today can be the first day toward your positive process of change if you want it to be.

*Do you have to work on acceptance of self?

Chapter Four
Acceptance in the Mirror Exercise

*****

During *your process of change* it is important that you are comfortable with all of you. That includes being okay with how you look on the outside while working on accepting you on the inside.

The *Acceptance in the Mirror Exercise* is meant to assist you in your journey toward self-acceptance. You can find in the mirror the tools that can help you tell your story. Acceptance starts with you being able see that moving into your purpose requires full attention to every part of you, and that includes being able to look at all of you and be confidant with what you see.

This exercise gives daily instructions over a months' time that will walk you through exercises that you will do with a mirror. There are tips provided along the way that will help you get through each week, so it's important that you complete each of the steps in the order that it is presented.

So while you have committed to positive change, be serious about the opportunity ahead to acknowledge and point out all of the things that are beautiful about you. You deserve this. Now let's get started.

Step 1

1. Take a watch or timer, pen and pad, and go to your private space with a mirror (body length if possible).
2. Remove all of your clothes (Yes, all of them) and stand in front of the mirror for three minutes.
3. Look at the reflection of all of you front and back. (You can make faces!)
4. When three minutes is up, immediately write down your feelings, thoughts, and emotions.
5. Say out loud, "I forgive myself for the wrong decisions that I have made and for my wrong doings. I forgive myself for neglecting me and for self-sabotaging myself. I forgive myself for any role that I played in ending relationships that were important and should be mended." (You should take as much time as needed to work through any emotions that you may have).
6. Say out loud "I must start to work on forgiving anyone who has ever abused or hurt me." This step may be really hard for some depending on the severity of the pain caused or how long it has been since

any abuse has occurred. But it is a necessary step toward your self- healing and growth. Trust that you will and can move to that necessary place of forgiveness. In *positive self-change*, know that you have to.

7. Say out loud, "I love myself because I know that I am loved and I promise to say it every day until I believe it. I promise to accept me and I promise to work on upgrading me to my standards."

8. Record your feelings, thoughts, and emotions.

9. Your homework every day for the next week will be to repeat, "I love myself because I know that I am loved." You don't have to be in front of the mirror to say this, just remember to say it.

10. Wait one week before moving to Step 2.

Step 2

1. Take a watch or timer, pen and pad, and go to your private space with a mirror (body length if possible).
2. Remove all of your clothes, (Yes, all of them) and stand in front of the mirror for three minutes.
3. Look at the reflection of all of you, front and back. (You can make faces!)

When three minutes is up, immediately write down your feelings, thoughts, and emotions.

4. After completing the three points, say out loud, "I love myself because I know that I am loved."
5. Look at the notes you took previously and compare them to the new notations that you just made. Highlight what made you laugh or cry, grimace or frown.
6. Wait three days, and go to Step 3.

Step 3

1. Take a watch or timer, pen and pad, and go to your private space with a mirror (body length if possible).
2. Remove all of your clothes (Yes, all of them again) and stand in front of the mirror for three minutes.
3. Look at the reflection of all of you, front and back. (You can make faces!)
4. Increase your time in the mirror to five minutes. After the five minutes have elapsed, record your feelings, thoughts, and emotions. This time do not compare your notes!
5. Write down what you like about yourself when you look in the mirror.
6. Focus on one thing that you will dedicate to showcase about yourself. If you have a hard time finding something that you like about your reflection, one of your goals will be to find one thing that you can focus in on your face that if you could, you would embellish to make stand out.
7. Try to showcase your new embellishment until the next step in the exercise. Stick to something that is inexpensive or easy to change. An example could be using a new eyeliner or eye shadow, a different color

lipstick, a hat, a new hairstyle, or a new style of earring. The options are endless!

8. Say out loud, "I love myself because I know that I am loved."

9. Wait one week, then move on to step 4.

Step 4

1. Take a watch or timer, pen and pad, and go to your private space with a mirror (body length if possible).
2. Remove all of your clothes (Yes, all of them.) You should be more comfortable with this part of the process by now.
3. Look at the reflection of all of you front and back. (You can make faces!)
4. Increase the time in the mirror to eight minutes.
5. Record your thoughts and emotions, and compare them to all of the notes taken since the first phase of the exercise. Record what feature you have been focusing on over the last week and any thoughts about how you feel about the changes.
6. Wait two days and move to Step 5.

Step 5

1. Take a watch or timer, pen and pad, and go to your private space with a mirror (body length if possible).
2. Remove all of your clothes. (Yes, you know the drill.)
3. Look at the reflection of all of you, front and back. You can make faces.
4. Increase the time in the mirror to ten minutes.
5. Write down your feelings, thoughts, and emotions. This time, write down if you looked forward to doing the exercise since the two days that were skipped, or if you were relieved that you didn't have to do the exercise. Be sure to write down all of your reasons why or why not.
6. Don't forget to say out loud, "I love myself because I know that I am loved."
7. Wait one week and move on to Step 6.

Step 6

1. Take a watch or timer, pen and pad, and go to your private space with a mirror (body length if possible).
2. Remove all of your clothes.
3. Look at the reflection of all of you, front and back.
4. Complete the time in the mirror for ten minutes again this week.
5. If you feel you don't want to do it, dig down deep inside and make sure you complete the exercise. Record your feelings, thoughts and emotions.
6. Remember to Say out loud, "I love myself because I know that I am loved."
7. Wait two days and move on to Step 7.

Step 7

Meet with a very special person in your life. Someone you really trust, be it your significant other or a best friend. Explain that this is not meant for their input, you invited them to just listen. (This may be difficult for some as you will be saying these most intimate feelings to someone for the first time. So make sure that you are in a private setting).

Discuss the mirror exercise that you have been doing and read all of your notes that you have recorded from day one out loud. Pay attention to how you are feeling in the moment.

1. Take a ten minute break to collect yourself and record your thoughts, feelings and emotions.
2. Explain that you are finished with their participation, and continue on with your day.
3. Wait until the next day and move on to Step 8.

Step 8

1. Take a watch or timer, pen and pad, and go to your private space with a mirror (body length if possible).
2. Do the mirror exercise for three minutes wearing shoes, jewelry, and underwear. Record your feelings, thoughts and emotions.
3. Look at the reflection of all of you, front and back.
4. Make note of what has changed about you since you have begun this exercise and what those around you have noticed about you and your change since your embellishments.

Say out loud, "I love myself because I know that I am loved."

Congratulations! You have completed the *Acceptance in the Mirror Exercise*!

By this point you should have gotten used to looking at yourself in the mirror and have figured out what you like and what you don't like about what you see when you look in the mirror. It is so important in your *process of change* that you be willing to open up and do something different to discover the things about you that you never took the time to see or evaluate before.

You can take this opportunity while going through this mirror exercise to realize and accept that you *are* everything that you see in front of the mirror and it is *you*. You should also take note, that the entire time that you were doing the mirror exercise your daily life and routines didn't change much throughout the past month. You still had to show up at work, and you still had to take care of yourself or your family.

I say this to show that we can work toward our positive change without causing a big disruption, or investing hundreds of dollars to get to the place of self-acceptance. It just takes time, commitment and dedication.

So by the end of this month when you have finished the mirror exercise you should make note of these four things about yourself:

1. You control you and the decisions that you make.
2. There are small things like this exercise that you can do to figure out how to love and accept yourself during *your positive process of change.*
3. When you work on accepting who you are while looking at yourself in the mirror, you start to believe it, you become comfortable

with you and it becomes your truth, no matter what you look like. You will know that how you feel about you is directly related to how you treat others and how others feel that you should be treated.

4. When you give you the time and attention that you deserve, you will find inside of that mirror that your true beauty is in the eyes staring back.

Now that you can work toward living in your world where you have unconditional acceptance of self, you could work on giving that to others.

Chapter Five
The Process of Change

"If you live your life knowing that Faith is your friend and Grace is your promise, you will realize that you've come equipped from day one with everything that you need to be free in your purpose."

*****

And so, a little birdie once told me that, "In this journey of life, we must think carefully about what we decide to bring along with us on our travels."

Albeit, the bags of stuff that we carry with us may change from time to time, that which defines who we are should always accompany us no matter where we go as these are the things that help to validate the testament of our characters. I am talking about the essential items of life that together with our values are necessary to help us stay on the right track as we move along. Things like the gifts of love, the gifts of courage, and the gifts of patience, the gifts of acceptance, the gifts of forgiveness, and the prize of faith.

These should be the things that we keep around to remind us and to help us set the ground rules when deciding how and why we make the choices that we make. To move about your existence as if life will just take care of itself without you encompassing these fundamentals on some level, will eventually turn your lightweight shoulder bags into the heaviest unwanted luggage that is sure to weigh you down over and over again right into your future.

If you will trust and commit to this journey, you could begin your progress toward living your life the way that you have dreamed of living it for years. If you have always wanted to dance, go find dance studio and take lessons. If you have love computers go enroll in a computer course. Even if you have already tried before without much success, you can start over from scratch and give it another try.

Even if after every time you try to move forward with optimism, you seem to come right back to the same negative place where you swore you would never go again; you should still get back up and start from the beginning with a positive attitude.

Though at times it may seem as if you are just treading water when you really want to be moving upstream, you can start to change things for yourself by taking a chance to get out of your comfort zone and commit to trying new things.

For most of us when it comes to change,

not only are we resistant to the reality of the new circumstances, but purposely or not, we allow the unknown to paralyze the opportunity for us to get the *'Blessing in the lesson'*. Our reluctance to try new things can result in missing out on new experiences.

And so, if right now you are sick and tired of being around people who you don't really see as helpful to the vision of your future then, move away from that circle and start to associate with like-minded people who will route for your success every time.

During this process it will be important to continue to plan what you want for yourself. It's not too late to complete some of those dreams.

Because we have all done things in our past that we are not proud of, and we have all accepted things that we knew we shouldn't have, we have to be okay and know that mistakes are necessary for us to learn and define what it is that we like or dislike. The job that is left for you to do is to focus on those things about you that need fine tuning so you can say that you have tried.

Because change will take us to a place that allows those parts of us that we are not comfortable with to begin to show, we have to welcome and nourish the new parts of us that we have discovered immediately in order to fight the urge to push them back inside.

Now get serious with your choices and re-create your daily, weekly, and yearly schedules to reflect the changes that you desire and move forward as if your life depends on it. Because it does.

Chapter Reflection

What are three things that you wanted to accomplish but didn't?

Are some of those things that you wanted to do still doable?

Chapter Six
Live it with Courage

"In courage you can learn to trust the you that has gotten you up this hill thus far. Know that if you have something to say, it is very important that you find a way to say it because you never know how your words can help or change the life of another. After all, as it has been told, the first words ever spoken created the path of existence for everyone thereafter."

*****

I am glad that you are with me because when it comes to courage during your *positive process of change*, I am talking about choosing to stay in that place of beauty for yourself for every bit of time that it takes before you move on to the next.

Courage is what separates the ordinary from the great, the great from the extraordinary, and the extraordinary from the legendary! Courage is our very own high priced tailor made suit given to us in this life to help us restore and renew our Faith in everything that we do.

It is the thing that helps us to continue to dream for the things that we don't have or that we can't see, so that we can keep the energy and the momentum to climb to places that seem unreachable. Courage is about owning the work that you have accomplished up to this date, and holding yourself accountable for the goals that you set, no matter what is waiting for you down the road.

I mean to say that in courage you must be brave enough to get comfortable with challenge at a new and higher level and believe that since there are so many different shapes of courage, you must take the time to learn what it looks like personally. Then you will be able to see when imposters show up as the presence of fear, doubt, envy or betrayal.

Trying to skip past this step in our climb towards personal success is one of the main reasons that most of us take a longer time at getting to know our level of self-worth.

Let me explain.

Because we can be quick to second guess ourselves about who we are or what we can do, we put to sleep that inner part that understands us the most. Being courageous enough to know that you are capable of leading yourself into the unknown, even if no one else is on your cheering squad but you, is what courage embodies.

People who are serious about what this life has to offer them as they push forward to strive for their goals, understand that the funny feeling that creeps up your stomach when you are nervous or afraid, has the big ticket prize awaiting them on the other side, every time.

Take for instance professional tennis or track competitors. They get up everyday rain or shine, regardless of aches and pains, determined to be faster and better than they were the day before. No excuses. They do whatever it takes to make sure that they do not miss a minute of practice because they know that a missed chance at growth could be the difference between just qualifying and claiming the number one spot on game day. Professional champions train fearlessly and stop at nothing short of their personal best so that they are victorious at competition time!

That's what I wish for those of us who are deciding to make this change toward our personal growth. In order to be the very best at us, we have to decide to reflect everyday on our accomplishments of yesterday, celebrate them, and strive for more today and tomorrow.

As we talk about courage, I am reminded of a friend that I knew, an insurance salesman, who was faced with losing his job because of his low end of the year sales. Worried about the possibility of not having a job at the start of the new year, he knew that he had to come up with something new and out the box to show his employer that not only was he a great salesman, but that he could be the best and most profitable asset to his business.

Taking a step back to remind himself that since he already knew how to be a successful salesman, he had to change his approach while remembering not to forget all of the years of training that he had.

Although he was terrified to go at it with new strategy and no one to guide him on how to do it, he came up with an idea for a new approach to getting clients to sign up for insurance. During the middle of his first office visit of a potential client, in noticing pictures of the client's family and precious keepsakes that were meticulously placed on the desk and walls, he decided to try to appeal and tug at the heart string of the client by inquiring about all of the different people in the photos.

He made it a point to highlight the importance of making sure that his wife and family would be protected if things didn't go as he planned. The salesman honed in on the lifestyle that the client had created for his family and reminded him how difficult it would be for his family if he were not here to continue to contribute.

Before he left the office that day he had

convinced the client to purchase the highest policy in the history of the company. That was the first of many clients that he got to sign up for insurance in his climb towards becoming the first multi-million dollar insurance salesman in his region.

Because he decided to look fear straight in the eye and took the courage to look inside and trust that he could go back to the basics of who he was, he was able to get it done. Even with the odds stacked against him. This is what living in courage is. Being determined to figure out what the element of success is for you, even when you can't recognize what it looks like.

Having the guts to trust in the new experience is what you have got to remember. You must put to rest any doubt of what you can do to reach the height of your *positive process of change* and sustain your position there.

When we talk about courage, it is about reaching out as far as your dreams can take you, and then broadening your imagination to reach even further. When you decide to be willing to believe that you can do anything that you put your heart, mind and soul to do you will begin to move out of that old way of thinking; thinking that was someone else's way of doing things or derived from someone else's definition of you.

No matter the cost you will incur, or the

relationships that you may lose from those who do not support you, you must not look back on your mistakes of yesterday. That is courage in your process of change. Gaining that element of unstoppable determination that will take you from wondering if you can do it, to knowing that you can do it is courage.

Start to embrace challenges and figure you out the same way that you figure out everything else that you want to learn about. But this time, research you!

Become what courage is so that you can be accurate in your definition. Put your name in front of the word courage and write it in a sentence. Branch out and get a conversation scheduled with a teacher or a CEO of a company to get some pointers on what they did to push back the crippling effects of fear in order to become successful. Go to a library and read encouraging books about successful people to elevate your understanding of triumph. Do whatever you need to everyday to preset your mind-o-meter to excellence and then do it!!

If you are not the person on the outside that you are inside, stop being scared to step up and start to show it. It is important for your *positive process of change* that you don't allow fear to keep you hidden. Because if you let it, fear will become the heavy weight barrier between you and your life's purpose.

When in fear we feel defeated and we forget about ourselves and our goals. We throw our plans out of the window and allow countless hours of worrying to take up the encouraging space in our minds. During your *positive process of change*, start to recognize that everything that you put energy towards will manifest itself, and that includes fear. If you repeatedly say that you are scared of something, then you will continue to attract the negativity of fear toward that thing.

Now is the time to embrace and be excited of the unknown toward the path of your purpose and your destiny! If you repeatedly stay encouraged about new things and exude positivity, then positive experiences and results will welcome you.

Know that the rest of your life is right there next to where your courage is waiting for you. The universe will acknowledge your sincerity and help you realize that you were chosen to do it!

Whatever it is you want for you, dedicate yourself to gathering the tools to do all that you can to accomplish what you set out to do. When you decide to do this for yourself, you are guaranteed another chance to show up to see the positive change that you deserve. Even if you make mistakes and miss out on an opportunity you have to remain positive and open to another chance.

Believe in, "If at first you don't succeed; you must try, try, and try again, until you do."

That is courage.

Chapter Reflection

*The universe is interested in what you've got. Decide to be brave enough to do you.

*What are you afraid of that is stopping you from moving forward with your purpose?

*What do you want to do differently now that you are in your process of change?

Chapter Seven
You and Change

*****

We may have at one time or another gotten ourselves in situations that we knew the moment after for whatever reason we said yes, we should have said no.

I believe that we have to make a serious effort to understand that we all have the opportunity to correct or face the wrongs that we have made. What's important to remember is that neither of us was given a crystal ball with the correct moves or answers to life's questions.

So if we fail at something we can believe that we've done all that we know up to that moment. And we have to remember even though *change is inevitable* and a serious part of the cycle of life, change can be challenging therefore, is not a popular subject for all of us.

Although all around us we are given examples showing us how important change is, we resist the thought of stepping out of our norm. Everyday our earth changes, our landscape changes, our styles change, and every few months our seasons change to move toward its purpose; all for the chance to glow at the new.

Look at the trees. (Yes, a little about the

trees. Well, it is in the title.) The scheme of colors that they give us are made to provide us inspiration every day to dream and create. Take the time to witness all of nature and its magnificently diverse pallet.

We know that trees void of water and nutrients, or space in which to flourish, will eventually shrivel and die. And if we pay attention, especially to the trees when they are in their blooming and shedding stages, we can understand how we like nature, are given the chance to grow, and be brave enough to show up again every few months, stronger and richer in who we are.

If we don't continue to feed our minds with education and learning, or allow our souls the freedom of our expression, then we can begin to feel like we will shrivel up and die as well.

Change can be hard, and I understand that. So of course when the change is unexpected and the event throws a curve ball that rearranges our already solidified plans for Monday and Tuesday, our instinct is to fight to keep things as they are. And, that's normal to a point.

But again, in this conversation, I want you to remember that since some change is going to happen rather we prepare for it or not, we should be in heads up mode for the most part to allow some wiggle room for the growth of the new season. Let's think about it for a second.

We have all gotten accustomed to living our lives by schedules and appointments; even the ones that we make months ahead of time and are expected to keep. We are all on auto pilot for the most part, so adjusting to any change can shake things up. Especially in these times where technology keeps our schedules planned and ready to remind us.

We've got mobile phones, planners, digital calendars with our favorite catchy little ring tones, all capable of keeping appointments for years ahead. We get up, exercise, get the kids on their way, head off to school or work, think of dinner all day, and make a stop at the grocery store on the way home, while talking on the cell phone listening to the latest from our best friend, mom, sister or spouse. We do this all while at the same time preparing the minutes for the meeting the next day. Whatever your schedule is, it's the way you do your thing every day. We get into a groove and after a short time where we are productive, we naturally get comfortable with the position.

Here is where turning up the volume of our level of self-awareness should come into play, so that when the unexpected events do occur in our lives we will be sure not lose our way. We have to pay close enough attention to how our schedules or commitments effect the way we handle all areas in our lives. So instead of getting caught up in the heaviness of the normal, in change we can remember the ABC's of problem solving or the 123's of the process of decision making to help us adjust.

And I will tell you why. Because in between any time of change we all get comfortable with ourselves, and rightfully so, because we have a serious belief system that allows us to process, react, and decide on which way to turn in life situations. Especially if we are confident that we have mastered our coping strategies that have helped us to be successful at overcoming tough obstacles in the past.

Our belief system is the element within us all that is either strong enough to help prepare us for a battle, or is the part of us that is so quiet that we cannot hear it when it's trying to lead us when things get too loud. So what I am proposing is that we work on getting to a comfortable place within ourselves, and learn how to stay there for a while so that our belief system will mature to a point that we will continuously have a healthy result in change.

Some of us have to begin to look at how we arrive at the conclusions that we do when we are handling our finances, or relationships; our parenting, or even something as simple as what we will prepare for dinner, so that whatever happens at the end of the day, we are okay with the result, and its finality will serve as the reality that it is supposed to be.

Even for the strongest, change can be difficult because it is easy for us to be comfortable in what we know, assuming that things will just work themselves out without us having to put in the new work with the new chapter in change. No pun intended... Because remember, even you, are also written in the plans of the Divine.

Chapter Reflection

*****Where are you at now with change and what
you need to work on for yourself, your family
or your relationships?*

Chapter Eight
A little bit on You and Anger...

*"Anger places limitations on our inner peace.
When sitting in anger we lose our ability to be
free in it."*

*****

This is the chance for us to discuss that with courage and acceptance we can work through anything. Right?

So for this conversation on anger, I implore you to put your defenses away before you read more into this chapter and allow yourself this opportunity to explore another side of you. Especially if you are the person who when upset, gets caught off guard, or when your back is up against the wall, loses control and goes straight from level 1 to 10 bypassing everything logical in between.

What we have to discuss is how you feel when you are angry or how you feel when you are disrespected. Because what is often missed when a situation goes awry or when personalities clash is the opportunity to assess what's actually going on before we go straight to anger. I'm not talking about being against feeling angry or upset if something warrants it. I am just saying that because anger is one of the emotions out of many that we all experience that is usually misunderstood, it's going to be important in your *process of positive change* you see you and anger differently.

Anger should be understood as it is intended to be a response to feelings of unhappiness that we experience in an unpleasant circumstance or situation. But anger is one of the more powerful emotions and is often used under the wrong pretense. Like anything that has power, it is very easy for us to let it take control. Because it's usually the easiest to turn on, we make anger the opponent against patience and acceptance, instead of a working partner in conflict or in times of disappointments.

Within your *positive process of change,* it is imperative that you work on how you express other emotions like sadness, fear, guilt, envy, and shame, for a few. Paying attention to how we mask our emotions is going to be key in order to figure out how to change our reactions to life circumstances.

Some of us cry when we get angry, or stomp around. Some get silent and act as if nothing is bothering them, which by the way can be just as damaging to someone who gets disruptive in anger. Then, some of us get so angry that we lash out and get violent then try to manipulate or blame the very next person who comes walking into the room.

I am in no way saying that we should not get angry. By all means there will be times when we will. However, if it is the case that you have accepted you and your anger up until now, no matter the damage that you have caused, starting today, I want you to get to know yourself and your anger so that you can keep you and your anger in check.

Since some have never learned how to deal with or been held accountable for all of our actions in and around anger, we have let our emotions be the excuse for us to justify our behaviors. Which in almost all cases turns out to be the incorrect way to handle the situation for everyone involved, because it gives the person a reason to get behind the anger and hang out as they can feel safe there.

But in change, you can recognize yourself in anger and realize that those strong behaviors are only smoke screens that have gotten you to a point where anger is now a part of your identification. This is what you must begin to change about yourself, because usually people remember the ugly things that you have done and will often use those things to define you quicker than they will speak about the good things about you.

With that said, you can cut yourself some slack if this is something that you have to work on because by the time that most of us are adults, we express our anger in the way that we have been allowed to express anger our entire lives.

And let's just put it all out there since we are talking about it. We all have that one person in our family or social circle, where when something is about to go down someone else in the room says, *"Oh, goodness. Here we go. You know how they get!"*

But if you're the person that does not know how to censor your anger, you get in your comfort zone while everyone else is getting uncomfortable. Since anger has been the vehicle on which some of us are used to cruising through life to get out of most situations, everybody surrounding that person has also become accustomed to moving things around or avoiding the confrontation, instead of dealing with the real situation at hand.

A lot of times what looks like anger in someone who goes off at the smallest of things can really be a reaction or a mask to hide feelings of fear, hurt, sadness, or confusion. And, believe it or not, can also be symptoms of an undiagnosed medical condition.

This is not so uncommon because most of

us hide our true feelings and are afraid to show what our real emotions are. We fear what the responses of others might be. In reality, what we desperately want is to be in control of some area of our lives, or at the very least in control of our emotions. When we are not allowed to exhibit the result that we want to because we get upset, our real emotions becomes dispositioned as Anger and comes out to hurt others as much as we are hurting.

But again, during your *positive process of change* if you and your anger sound anything like a situation described above, you must begin to open yourself up to learning how you can make different choices when you are upset. It's all about the new way of thinking. Anger, if one is not taught how to process it correctly will block your spiritual growth and take away all sense of comfortableness that you have in the 'who' that you really are.

Before today, if you were someone who repressed your anger by holding it all in, your anger was mismanaged and would be released by you probably fighting the tears, beating somebody up, or engrossing yourself in somebody else's business to cover your pain. Let's understand that for the most part the misuse of anger is a learned behavior. With determination you can learn to correct your responses to you and your feelings when you get upset so that you can reshape what anger is in your life.

Anger left unchecked, will leave you all alone wondering why. Living in anger can take your power away to think rationally and causes the loss of important relationships. Staying in anger and holding grudges destroys your peace and leads to suffering, disappointment, even embarrassment.

In your *positive process of change*, you must learn to change your thought process when things don't go as planned and understand that what you are really feeling can be simply feelings of unhappiness that will subside. Going forward you must start to deal with the real issues behind why you are so angry.

If you have been abused by someone, or when you are hurt or upset with yourself for allowing something to take place that you shouldn't have, it's time to confront that situation. You have to start with forgiveness and give yourself permission to do what you need to do during that time of pain in order to not let negativity take the place where healing should be.

It is a fact that anger comes along with resentment or disappointment. It is imperative to your health that you choose to seek peace and tranquility, even when you are hurting. Notice it and accept it, so that you will be better for it.

Just like any other trait or characteristic, anger changes us, inside and out. When you let anger take the lead it changes your body temperature, increases your brain waves, and distorts your thinking. If you are the person who allows yourself to get to that highest threshold of anger when it grows to an uncontrollable state, you can have an experience that you may not even remember once your vital signs calm down and come back to normalcy.

Let's pause and take a few moments to remember the last time that you got really upset about something or at someone. A situation where if you thought long enough about it right now, you can still see clearly the day and the events that happened. I'll give you another minute to go there.

Okay, now that you are almost at the point where you are starting to relive that moment, check your heart rate. Has it started to beat a little faster ever so slightly? Well, it should be because of the normal physiological effects that happens to all of us when we get angry. It is the connection between our minds, body, and what we are feeling.

The human body's natural instinct is to go into protection mode and tries to deal with the erratic pulsations of our heart. When this happens we begin to feel a change in our body as our blood pressure rises and our breathing starts to become more rapid. Some of us may begin to sweat, get uncomfortable and become frightened at these events happening inside of us that we cannot immediately get under control. That is the moment that we can allow anger to be the boss of us.

But, we all have a 'self-check" mechanism that is just one of the ways to innately help us remain focused when we get anxious. I'm referring to those inner nudges that are given to us to use as our own special GPS system to help guide us through life.

If you think about it, we all look consciously or unconsciously to that inner something, especially during moments of confusion or at times when we need reassurance to give us what we need to move forward. We have to trust in it during our *positive process of change* so that we can redirect our behavior.

Your goal is to change the way that you feel about anger so that you can expose what you may be using to re-traumatize yourself from the events of your past. Remember until you get that this is what you have been doing to yourself when you are upset, this may seem normal to you.

Going forward, know that you have the freedom of choice to change the way that you feel about your past in anger. You can put the work in right now to change the way you present yourself when angry.

Chapter Reflection

*Managing your anger will take more effort than time. Your dedication is what's needed.

*Do you see yourself in this discussion as having issues with how you deal with your anger?

*Are you ready to seek assistance if needed to help you with how you deal with your anger?

Chapter Nine
Anger Exercise

The power in controlled breathing...

Sometimes when we are in the heat of an argument or when we find ourselves in a situation where we have to react on the spot, we can lose focus. When this happens, tempers can flare, we can use all sorts of tactics as a shield for us until we gain back our composure. Which can be easier said than done for some.

The point of this exercise is to give you a tool that you can use when or if you need a few moments to control your emotions so that you can deal clearly with any situation.

What we know is that when you are in control of your breathing you are in control of your heart rate, your level of anxiety, and most importantly, you remain in control of you.

When you feel yourself getting angry or struggle with keeping control of any of your emotions, you should practice this exercise as much as possible so that when you are in a situation you are prepared to be in control.

1. Take a deep breath and start counting in descending order from ten out loud. Close your eyes if you can and think of something calming or try to picture one of

your favorite things.

2. Take another deep breath and exhale then say nine out loud.

3. Take another deep breath and exhale then say eight out loud.

Repeat this process in continuing descending order.

4. Try to think of how you can imagine yourself handling the current situation if you were in control.

Once you reach one, take one last deep breath and relax into yourself. Let your body feel the calmness that is happening.

After you have completed this exercise through to the last step, if you still feel your heart is still racing, repeat the exercise from the beginning.

The power in walking away...

It is true that some of us get over the top when we are upset or angry based on our past and our personalities. So I wanted to talk a little bit more about how we can change our behaviors when we feel ourselves getting out of control.

When you feel your emotions starting to get further away from your baseline when you get angry, pay closer attention to what you are thinking as the moments within the situation deepens. Are you starting to feel intimidated, or disrespected? Do you feel the need to start to defend yourself or protect someone you care about?

Pinpointing those things are important because how we react can be based on the severity of the premise behind the situation. So, before you go past that point, you can decide if this is one of the times that warrants your response, or if you should just walk away.

I know this may seem like a simple task and for some situations it will not be appropriate. But if you are really going to put your best effort into accepting responsibility for yourself when you become angry, you have to be open to try different approaches at learning how to calm yourself before you react. Walking away from certain situations does a few things:

1. It allows you time to act as a mature adult

would and gives you time to think of the consequences of your actions.

2. It allows you to react according to the situation at hand.
3. It allows you the chance to determine if your time is even worth commenting or reacting at all.
4. And mainly, it allows you the chance at maintaining full control over you.

Again, the goal for you during your *process of change* is to fine tune you. And if anger is a big issue that you have to work on personally, then I say that you do whatever is necessary to improve you.

Chapter 10
Interlude on "Gratefulness"

"Being thankful for what you have and remembering the less fortunate will bring you fulfillment, it will make you smile."

*****

Every day, the moment that I come home I say a separate prayer thanking Him for my special space and for all of the little things that I have. It may seem simple to some, but for me it continues to be my sign that I have another day in Grace. I'll tell you why.

When I was in high school just before graduation, there was an educator who told me that I was not going to go any further than my high school career. She specifically stated that because I didn't score very well on the SAT's, and since my family didn't have the money and/or the connections to help me get further my education, that I should stop thinking about college. She continued on to say that I would be better off looking into a program to learn a trade so that I'd be able to take care of myself.

Although this was discouraging for me to hear, it didn't stop my thirst and my pursuit for knowledge and higher education. What that educator didn't know was that the seed of education had been planted in me and my siblings so deep at an early age by an older aunt, who was not only an educator, but was also a principal. From the position that my aunt held in academia, she made sure that we understood the necessity of and the power gained by continuing education beyond high school.

My aunt gave me and my sister's books as gifts so that we would know how to read very well at a young age. We soon began to better understand the meaning of the words that lay within the covers of the many books that we read and we began to own that it was our responsibility to apply what we learned through the written word.

Being that our passion for reading inspired our passion for writing, my sisters and I promised that since our parents didn't go far in education that we would go as far as we could.

And this is one of the reasons why I am grateful. Because even though those negative words could have caused me to lower the expectations that were set for me, I didn't accept them and continued to stay focused on my education.

I know that there are individuals and families who find difficulty with being able to grasp hold of the opportunities afforded them, because of the barriers facing them every day that they can't see past. So I want to be an inspiration to others to show that if I found a way not to allow those obstacles that have presented themselves throughout my life deter me from achieving the goals that I have set for myself, they can too.

Some have never been afforded the opportunity to graduate from high school or even to walk onto a college campus, which I struggle with because I know that the institution of learning is so powerful and instrumental.

Because it is true that in higher education you are sure to learn something every day just by showing up as you find yourself surrounded by people from all over the world eager to share their experiences and cultures. In education you have an educator whose job is to offer you a space to grow and learn by encouraging you towards change every day, and expecting you to come prepared to meet them with your challenges in tow.

Along my journey I was able to talk with some about the importance of education and about not giving up if the road seems to run out on them. It humbled me and made me so grateful to stand in the moment with a young man or woman who was so thankful that I had helped them see a brighter outlook into education.

I eventually learned that the *Blessing in my lesson* was for me see that there is always going to be someone in a situation worse than I. The key is to remember that before we lie down, wherever we are to sleep, that we did what we could in that day to help someone else. And also that not only is having our own space important to being who we are, but being able to have, at the end of each day, a place to call our own is truly a gift.

I still give thanks every day when I walk into my room. I say a prayer that those unfortunate will get at least one moment through the night to be able to dream and feel His love.

Chapter Reflection

*What are you grateful for?

*Do you give back or volunteer in your community?

Chapter 11
Live it In Love…

"It is true that Love is a partner in the essence of time because of its tenacity to go the distance."

*****

Let's remember that another commonality amongst all of us is the desire and the need to be loved. It does not matter what you choose to love, or who you choose to love. Love is missed when it's gone and welcomed with open arms when it comes back.

Because love endures all things and is awesome in its power, it is easy to grab hold of and hang on to for wherever the ride will take us. And rightfully so, especially when we are in the beginning of a new love experience and everywhere we go people are singing about love, talking about love, reading books about love, and will rush out to stand in long lines waiting for the latest movie about love.

Within your *positive process of change*, it is going to be vital that you get to a place where you know what love can do for you and in turn, what you can do for love.

Love needs time to get an identity.

Love needs time to be respected.

And since there are high expectations placed on the concept that 'love' will work it all out, we need to give ourselves the space to allow love to bloom in its own time.

Moving to a place of accepting how love will play its part in our lives to our personal understanding of patience and maturity in love, is what it is going to take to ensure that you grow with the beauty of love before you claim or blame everything on it.

Sorting through past experiences or figuring out what lessons in love we should keep close to our hearts, as opposed to which ones we should put up on a shelf for safe keeping, is where in love you must get to in your *positive process of change.*

It is not really explained to most of us that just about everything that we do in life circles back to love in some way, and the way that we feel about love is how we give love. Up until today, if you were abused by love, you probably abused love, or have accepted that love will always abuse you.

Love is directly related to how we continue to choose the same type of person to have a relationship with even after we know for a fact that we should be looking for different qualities in the next person. Qualities that can come as close to our standards as possible, and, that can help validate our self-worth. Because we don't give ourselves time in between the last relationship to explore what went wrong or what wasn't right for us, we usually get right back out there trying to find the next one that will fill the void; instead of who will deserve us.

Going forward in love and in our *positive process of change*, we should be looking for love from someone who likes the same things that we like or who will love what you love either with you or for you even when you are not around. I am talking about all of the elements in a relationship that look and feel like love because it is love. Not something that feels like love just because it feels good.

Staying in a relationship and saying that it is love because he or she is compatible in the bed and can help you get feelings of bliss that you never thought could be possible, maybe because it is your first time feeling them, is not the relationship in love that you should be looking for.

We have to get to a point where we surround ourselves with companions, male or female, who are going to help us grow in our efforts to stay real with what is love and what it is not.

I am saying this because we all really want true love to show its face to us but it is easy to misconstrue what love should feel like when we experience something new. What we have to do is resist the urge to comparing it to the old.

In our *positive process of change*, you must begin to accept that the way you used to think or react to Love has got to be a thing of the past. You must open your heart to accept love.

In order to see how great you can be in love, you must change—which I understand is not easy to do. People, places, things, food, clothes, and most important, your attitude about the love of yourself and others.

Now, I know that this may sound lame or corny to some, but I also know that what you believe about yourself gives life and energy that you deserve and need. And, I believe if you truly put your energy into only the positive imagery of love, negative feelings of love will dissipate.

So whether you have completed the Acceptance in the Mirror Exercise or not, just say it. Yes. Right now! Say it today, tomorrow, and everyday going forward. *"I know that I am love because I am loved."*

Say it as many times as you need to until you start to believe it, and until you start to love how it sounds coming out of your mouth. Repeat it until you begin to feel the warmth of His grace, and until you know that you know, that you know, that you are loved.

It is when you believe it yourself that your life will have more meaning and your eyes will be opened to see all of this creation and that it is here for you and your place within it. Trust in it. You will begin to see that the way you start to open yourself up to love is the way that love will start to open up to you.

The essence of you will be evident to everyone and everything that you touch. You have to accept that you are loved even with all of your baggage, all of your self-doubt and even with all of your mistakes.

And what gives me the right to tell you anything about love or life or anything anyway? I can tell you that I found out about real love because I am one of the leaves that fell off my *Bare Naked Tree*. One of the leaves who decided to accept that I was deserving of the opportunity to live my purpose and shine in my promise, and one of the leaves who decided that my kind of love was only going to be defined by me.

Trust me, the feeling that you will get when you realize that accepting your gift of love is all that you need to do to start to live your life exactly as intended, will be indescribable. It will be all the confirmation that you need to step into your *Bare Naked Trees*.

Chapter Reflection

*Forgiveness, acceptance and love are key to our personal success.

*Do you say "I love you" to yourself and others that you love?

*Are you comfortable showing signs of love for others?

Chapter 12
Interlude on Love...
*****

Think back on a time when you were in love or around real love. You know the type of love where your heart beat so fast that it seemed to sing an unforgettable song. A song so strong that your eyes did its own dance.

Well I knew an elderly Native Indian woman whom I will call Mrs. Birdie that I would visit when I wanted to be around someone who was truly happy to see me.

I knew that she loved me by the way her eyes gleamed and sparkled when she saw me coming up the driveway. And it was even more evident when she would meet me at the door with a beautiful plate of her delicious soul food. I would walk around with a glow full of her warmth for days after. It was nice.

Mrs. Birdie was a small woman with a smile as wide as the ocean. She had a laugh that was so loud my chest would rattle if I sat close enough to her. She would share memories of when she was a child and would go to the Indian Reservation with her uncle to visit the Native Indian side of her family.

Mrs. Birdie was really proud to tell me about her aunts and uncles who would give her life lessons about courage, love, and lessons of self -respect.

On occasion, Mrs. Birdie would share some of her family recipes, and when she was feeling nostalgic she would show me pieces of fine antique jewelry that she helped make with her cousins.

On our last visit, although I didn't know it was going to be at the time, I had almost cancelled because it was a rainy day, and the driving conditions were treacherous. But since I'd had a funny feeling in my stomach earlier that day, I decided to bare the elements and go anyway.

When I pulled up to her house and saw Mrs. Birdie sitting on her porch smiling as if it was a sun shining day, I couldn't imagine being anywhere else but there. We sat on the porch and caught up with each other's lives since our last visit then oddly, a moment of silence was amongst us which was very unusual because Mrs. Birdie was never at a loss for words.

Finally, she leaned closer to me across the table and whispered, "I've been meaning to tell you one of the main reasons that it takes so long to find out that you need to love yourself first before you can live your purpose is because most of us are not taught to love ourselves first. We are not given the seed of courage in love to go out and face the world as we are."

"You see. I've seen in my old age that times have changed and the necessary lessons of love have been taken out of the teachings by us all. And as a result, our children are not taught how important it is for them to love themselves unconditionally first. So then when they are sent out into the world they are sure, and confident, and strong enough to know not to go digging under any old rock looking for any old thing that can keep a smile on their face for longer than an hour." She finished, grinning slightly.

"Because I was taught", she continued, "How to love myself first, I am proud to say that I have done what I was supposed to do for you. I knew the first moment that I saw you, you needed love, as your eyes were not sure of what was behind them.

You see, you used to come see this old lady because you thought that I needed company. But after a while you came out to be near me because you needed what I give to you. I'm not complaining, I'm just saying what it was."

"So remember this little girl," she said as she took hold of both of my hands, "Time and love is so much more precious than you understand. You've got to start spending time admiring you every day. You've got to thank Him all the time for his blessings and love and ask that HE keep you all the days long. You've got to ask Him to give you the wisdom and common sense not to bring your fool self out to see me in this weather again unless it's for my funeral!"

Bending over, Mrs. Birdie let out a huge whale of a laugh and waited for me to say okay before she continued with my life's most precious lesson.

"Hear me when I say," as she looked straight into my eyes. "A child who was not taught to love herself or himself turns into a woman or man who will do almost anything for someone who shows them love. No matter if the love they show is empty energy, it will be welcomed. But when you truly love yourself, truly, you will see the fake coming a mile up the road and can turn your head the other way from it."

I realized that she was right. I had been shown love in my life but had never been taught what it is to love myself unconditionally, or how to turn down a love that is not right for me. And the more I had thought about it, I couldn't recall but a few times where I had even had this type of conversation with anyone else.

"You see," Mrs. Birdie continued, "Most of us are so damaged by love that we give up on it before we can understand it. And it's because we have got to take the young children by the hand and teach them how to love: show them how to admire themselves. Tell them that they have to get used to looking at their own reflection every day. Tell them to stop and say hello to themselves when they walk by a mirror. Say, "Hello," and "I love you" to the person looking back. Because I tell you, the younger we start to understand true love of self, the easier it will be to believe in love and the easier it will be to accept love."

"Now I know that you have been working on change and all of that so, I want you to go home and put the finishing touches on loving yourself so you can show those who need help understanding what the gift of love can bring to their lives. I want you to take the time to look into the eyes of others and listen to people who need you to understand their story." And, "She added, "Smile baby. You are going to be okay because you are loved and know that I will always love you."

As I drove home that day I was shaken with emotion as it was a lot for me to take in. Thinking back on my own childhood, I began to understand what she meant when she talked about why it takes so long to find out what our purpose is. The love that was given to me by my family was genuine but I couldn't recall being shown examples of self-love the way Mrs. Birdie had spoken them.

So one day during my third editing of this chapter, as I was still trying to grasp all of the jewels of wisdom and words of encouragement that Mrs. Birdie had given me, I decided that I was going to try loving me every day to see what would happen. I was curious to see how different I would feel or how I would look through a more knowing point of view.

I thought every day about what Mrs. Birdie said to me about childhood teachings on love and decided that going forward I would give myself permission to move a little slower when choosing what is best for me and for my children.

I made the decision to remind myself every day that I matter, what I think about myself matters, and how I would move about growing the love that I had for myself matters.

And I kid you not, it was smooth sailing from then on. I fell so in love with myself that I was even getting on my own nerves from all of my excitement!

Even though I did not get the chance to visit with Mrs. Birdie after that day, I am sure she knew by that last hug we shared before I left her porch, that I would get the message loud and clear.

I tell this lesson of love because of what Mrs. Birdie meant to me and how she made the meaning of life and love so special to my life and purpose. I feel so blessed that I had the pleasure of spending all of those hours with her listening and learning about her history and ancestry.

It feels so good to know that she cared enough for me to not only *tell* me that I am loved, but also to *show* me that I am loved. And now I can proudly say I understand it was all so that I could tell you that you are truly worthy and you *are* loved as well.

Chapter 13
The Power Inventory Board
******

Now that we have worked our way to our *positive change*, let's try an exercise that can help us put a new perspective on the work that we have done toward our *Bare Naked Trees.*

Part of the way that I took power of the vision of my life's purpose, was to create my *Power Inventory Board.* The *Power Inventory Board* was created to act as a visual, a kind of platform to help guide me toward keeping a place for the moments that stood out for me when I thought about how I arrived at where I am today.

I knew during my *positive process of change*, in order for me to truly grasp the relevant events of my past and place them appropriately in my present and future life's script, I had to find a vehicle to see it all unfold.

Creating my *Power inventory Board* was an eye opening experience that made sense to me and brought it all together to become the aide I needed to help me prioritize my life and my dreams, as well as to set the foundation for my process of change. I started by writing down as many of my childhood dreams, along with my teen and adult experiences that I could attribute to having some connection to my goals. Not looking for any specific event or time, but just looking for whatever it was that represented me.

Once I was able to identify the events of my past that were repeated in all phases of my life learning, I saw cycles, patterns, and broken dreams that were sometimes caused out of necessity due to times of change. Some natural and some controllable.

During this process, I was able to see how certain elements surrounding my culture and upbringing, my ancestors, and life teachers played a vital part in the way that I chose my own personal goals. Now you can do the same for yourself and begin the real picture of your life's portrait to become a more accurate and truer representation of you.

Let's get started!

Power Inventory Board

(There will be 2 phases to this process. Remember this is a project that may take a few weeks depending on how much time you have to dedicate to it.)

*****

Phase 1

You will need a notepad, several sheets of large poster board, colored markers, stickers, time and patience.

1. Start by writing down your wants, needs, goals and dreams. Write the age or time in your life that you were when they first became important to you. If you recall, write the reasons that you haven't accomplished them.

2. Next, write if those dreams are still important to you, if you still can get them done now or in your future, and note how long it would take for them to come to fruition. Write how and what resources you would need to see them come true.

3. Arrange them in the order of which ones you could do within a year, then which ones might take three years, five years, and so on. Include everything. Travels, finances, savings, employment, family,

personal, professional, materialistic items.

Once you have completed the first steps above, put the list away and don't work on it for two weeks. Do not skip this step as you are going to need fresh eyes and an open mind to stay focused.

Phase 2

1. After the two weeks have passed, get your project out and reread what you wrote. You will see that some of the things on your initial list are not what you actually want to do anymore, or that they are not as important as they once were; so feel free to take away or add to the list.

2. Re-read certain chapters of *Bare Naked Trees* that were significant in helping you to put your goals into perspective. After you've done so, redo the list again, but this time write the list based on what you know is more realistic and more similar to the person you are working toward becoming now that you are in your *positive process of change*.

3. With your big poster board make four equal columns down the length of the board. Label each column by writing Wants, Goals, Purpose, and Promise, placing only one word across the top of each column.

4. Consult your list and use what you've written there to fill in the appropriate columns.

It's okay if it takes a while and/or if you have to redo this a few times until you get it looking how you want. This is okay and is the reason you have extra boards.

5. Once you have everything all written out it is time to create your actual Power Inventory Board.
6. Use your different colored markers, stickers, and whatever represents you to complete your board.
7. Hang your Power Inventory Board on an empty space on your wall or door where you can see it easily, permitting you the ability to read your board every day.
8. Lastly, start to trust and believe in it and the process.

Being able to see your own inventory every day will help shed light on the things in your life that are most important and what you could picture yourself doing. Be sure to celebrate you and mark off the completed accomplishments as you go along.

Although you may not find all of your life's answers within this one exercise, what you will know for sure is that your own *Bare Naked Trees* are promised.

Chapter 14
The Leaves that Fall off

"You must gather all of your leaves and put them up for safe keepings, as they are your cushions of life to be there to help catch you when you fall."

*****

Because not every leaf that falls off of a tree is lifeless or void of purpose, it is important to understand that some leaves get detached from their branches only because a strong wind has passed by and taken them along to fulfill another mission. Some of the leaves that end up on the ground are meant to provide us with hope wherever they land, because their main job has suddenly become to show us how to survive in the midst of a new environment as long as there is life within.

There are some leaves that stay on their tree until the tip of winter because of their personality and character. Those leaves are strategically selected to stay attached to their tree so they can continue to shine for someone whose light may still be dim, well into the changing season.

Where am I going with this?

Like leaves, we all come from our own tree with many different branches. We live day by day just trying to figure out how to create our own cycle of life that will be healthy enough to carry on to the next season, then the next, for many generations.

Within every season we know that there are leaves on trees with different colors, shapes and sizes which are each given their chance to bloom. Like us, we are given many chances to bloom and live out our purpose, even if we have to work through and within our diagnosis, or while healing from our addictions, or while surviving abuse.

Whatever obstacle that is yours, it is vital that you hold onto as many of the leaves from your tree as you can, because when you let go of your own leaves, or your own purpose or dreams, it is very easy to get lost in the pile and pick up someone else's.

In other words, we all have the opportunity to decide to hold onto and step into our purpose and make it happen, if only we can stay focused for as long as it will take us to get to it.

You have to understand that the gift of self-love and self-acceptance is so important to help you get down your road to celebrating all that you accomplish so that you can teach your children what it means to succeed, so then, they are secure enough to be free to dream.

Knowledge and education of self is our strongest power and allows one the permission and courage to talk and teach the things that are important about ourselves and our history.

I hope that *Bare Naked Trees* has been able to help you through your *positive process of change.* Whether you are a confident woman in the time of your life where all you might need to do is pick up a book to provide a few positive words in which to spend a quiet, relaxing afternoon; then, I hope *Bare Naked Trees* can help get you through your weekend.

If you are a lonely man looking for a comforting friend, I pray that *Bare Naked Trees* has given you your own new best confidante.

If you are someone struggling through a depressed state or an awkward time in your life, I hope *Bare Naked Trees* can give you the courage to seek needed resources that will help you remain focused or find your spark in life to prosper.

More than words, *Bare Naked Trees* is here for those who may find themselves in an unknowing place. For those who could use a little guidance to find the right track and to stay on it.

Bare Naked Trees is a reminder to you to place yourself in position to be ready to capitalize on the opportunities that change has to offer so that during your *positive process of change*, you have get the guts to stay in the change for as long as it takes for you to find your way around the newness. Give yourself permission to clumsily move around for a bit until you get comfortable enough to move about your new way with confidence.

Start to put what others may think about you in the garbage and know that it's not what may look good on the outside, but what is good for you on the inside, so that you will wear it well all the time. Even when you are *Bare Naked*.

Change will require you to step up, keep your promises to yourself every day, and prepare for truth in your growth so that during this *positive process of change* you will see that you are more powerful than you know. Start to listen to yourself when you are giving the good advice that you give to your friends and make sure to 'note to self' not to leave you out of the equation.

While preparing *Bare Naked Trees* for print, I would often stop and ask myself, "Am I worthy to write or suggest to anyone how to love or choose courage in their quest for self – acceptance?" As I too had doubts of my purpose.

But when I closed my eyes and turned to the next chapter and felt how fast my heart would pound when I thought of *Bare Naked*

Trees, or how my face would get flushed at the thought of the day when this project would be complete: I exhaled and smiled at what was waiting for me next to write.

Through this journey I have come to know the real meaning of what is means to 'stand'.

I am grateful that I was given the gift of courage to move forward with my passion and to reject the fear of failure that wanted to ruin my dream.

So if I can give you that gift to want to live in the world with love as your motivator, or to move with forgiveness, or acceptance and faith, then I know that I have gotten to the level of success that I believe was my purpose in *Bare Naked Trees*.

My prayer is that during your continued process of change, *Bare Naked Trees* will do the same for you as it did for my continued self-improvement. I am encouraged that these words will be a reminder for you to trust in yourself because you know you best, and you are the only one who knows what's right for you.

Remember, you are the only one who can set *your* standards, so embrace and nurture them to represent who you are. Know that *you* are the one who holds the key to unlock the chest to your personal happiness and success. If you *believe* in your truth, *you* have all you need to

embrace all of the branches of your own *Bare Naked Trees.*

Rachel S. Morrison is a native of Buffalo, NY, a mom of two handsome sons, and a beautiful grandson. Rachel enjoys dancing, running, writing, and relaxing beachside. Rachel has her MA Degree, and years of experience working to encourage self-empowerment. This is Rachel's first published work, but it is sure not to be her last as thoughts of Bare Naked Trees-Next Season is already working its way into existence. Also look for the release of her first full length novel *Fine as Wine Eyes*, as well as her work of poetry.

Rachel is owner of *The Power In We and is Co-Owner of Renewed Me* alongside her big sister, *RM.* You can catch the sisters launching their *Sisters To Sisters* Retreats and *Renewed Me* Series coming soon to a town near you!`